" *Dream the perfect thing but then go make the real thing* "

ELIZABETH GILBERT

MOTHER'S QUEST
INSPIRATION GUIDE

VOL.1 ENGAGE

SPARK YOUR E.P.I.C. LIFE

BY JULIE NEALE

Mother's QUEST
LIVE YOUR E.P.I.C. LIFE

SEIZE THE DAY.

LOVE YOUR PEOPLE.

HONOR YOUR GIFTS.

CREATED IN
LOVING MEMORY OF

Leslie Fischer

A lifelong friend who lived her E.P.I.C. life, especially as
she showed up fully for herself and her family during
her three year journey with pancreatic cancer.

CONTENTS

INTRODUCTION

MY QUEST

There are moments, like this one, when I glance back at my two children + therapy pup and it feels like everything has slowed down. Like I am literally breathing in the scene. And everything that made that moment possible rushes before my eyes.

I call these E.P.I.C. snapshot moments. The ones you want to bottle up.

My motherhood journey has not been easy.

Years of infertility, discoveries of learning and developmental differences for both of my boys, early intervention and specialists and IEP meetings, a pregnancy loss. And also pathways to transformation... tears and joy beyond what I thought was possible.

It's been a lot.

Along the way I lost myself.

And I also found parts of myself... a grit and resilience I never imagined possible.

A little over four years ago, I said "YES" to reclaiming all of myself and living according to a set of guideposts in what I now call my E.P.I.C. life. And on December 1st 2016, I launched Mother's Quest and the Mother's Quest Podcast as a 45th birthday present to myself.

In what I describe as a mid-life renaissance, Mother's Quest was my commitment to becoming the author of my story and the fullest expression of myself.

It became the container for creating opportunities for inspiration, coaching and community for me and other mothers. Through Mother's Quest, we could follow the lead of those a few steps ahead on the journey and we could also light the way for others. We could learn from one another and we would never have to feel alone.

Through these years, I've experienced so much. I've opened my eyes to injustice and stepped into activism in powerful ways. I've moved through new challenges with my children. I've coached other mothers through their own transformation. And have sat down to conversations on my podcast with some of the most inspirational change-making mothers around. Integrating the life lessons and the "challenges" my guests offer me at the end of each episode has enriched my life in incredible ways.

I wanted to capture some of the things I've learned on this leg of the journey. And do it in time for another birthday, 49...just on the threshold of becoming 50. Like the podcast, this book is a birthday present for me. And as always, it's an offering, an invitation for you too. As I say in my podcast opening "I created this for myself. But come along with me and you'll find some treasures of your own."

ABOUT THE BOOK

One thing that's always been on my epic life bucket list is to become a published author. I shared this with my teenager one day and he promptly challenged me to write my first book in 2020. Not one to shrink from a challenge given to me by my son, I found powerful guides in Lindsey Smith and Alexandra Franzen of the Tiny Book Course, an opportunity to go from idea to self-published book in 45 days, and decided to take the leap. I signed up for the course and invited other Mother's Quest members, with dreams of becoming an author themselves, to come alongside and create their own books too.

So, this little book in your hand, the first volume of four, is both decades in the making and also created in just a matter of weeks. It's the result of years of my Mother's Quest journey and also only days of curating and drafting. I followed the Tiny Book Course's invitation for "just good enough" and also reached out to key members of my team to assist. And I held the possibility that writing this book could be done in community, with ease and joy ...and it (mostly) was!

If you listen to the podcast, you know that the episodes are typically an hour in length. They are deep and reflective. They require you to press pause and settle in. My hope for this Inspiration Guide Series is to create a counter-balance to the podcast. An opportunity to dip a toe in on any page. To flip through to a practice and in a matter of minutes, feel inspired to try something new, or remember a truth you've always known in your life.

When determining what number of practices to share for the series, the number 18 came to me immediately.

Within the Jewish faith, 18 represents "chai" or translated from Hebrew to English "life." What better symbol to help us connect to strategies for living our fullest lives? So, there are four practices highlighted for each E.P.I.C. guidepost, and two practices for when you are "on the threshold" of a new chapter, that set the stage for them all. In Volume 1, we'll begin with "on the threshold" and then delve into the practices for the "E" in E.P.I.C. "engage mindfully with your children."

As you read, there will be sections with blank spaces to invite you to slow down and integrate the practices for yourself. If you'd like, you can write what comes up for you directly in the book in those spaces, you can choose to capture your thoughts in a separate journal, or you can just pause on the page and write nothing at all. The key is to give yourself permission to reflect in whatever way calls to you.

I've also curated special Mother's Quest Podcast episodes to help you go deeper in each practice. You can find these episodes on any of your favorite podcast apps and also you can read extensive show notes for each episode at the Mother's Quest website www.mothersquest.com/podcast.

I'm so thrilled that this first volume is here! I hold this wish for you and for me: that this book becomes a tiny companion with big impact on our E.P.I.C. life journeys. Whether we keep it on our bedside tables, or take it on the go, I hope we open it again and again and find something that lights our way to a more E.P.I.C. life each time.

LIVE YOUR
E.P.I.C. LIFE

A MANIFESTO IN THE MAKING

I remember the day I got clear that "E.P.I.C." was the life I wanted to live and created the E.P.I.C. framework with a napkin and a pen at my kitchen table.

It was midnight and I had been having conversations in a private group all day with Harmony Leanna Eichsteadt then of the Good Life Project team about what I was really trying to do with this vision I had for Mother's Quest. Harmony was reflecting back to me what she thought she heard..."You want to help mothers have more balance in their lives," she said. "You want to help them live better lives."

"No!" I remember typing emphatically in the comments, pounding the keyboard as I went. It's more than that! I want them to live their version of an "epic" life...the kind of life filled with all the things that matter most. A life where when you look back, perhaps when sitting on a porch with your grandchildren, you can tell your loved ones stories about all the things you did in your life, the experiences that shaped you, the challenges you overcame, and the difference you made.

I decided "epic," though not a perfect word, best captured what I was trying to express. But, there was more to it than this idea of the powerful "story" of our lives. I wondered whether it could also act as an acronym for all the things I was most on a quest for as a mother... the things that I think help us to live an epic life when we are raising our children.

So, I sat down with a napkin and a pen and wrote out the first letter of epic "**E**" and sure enough, **engaged** mindfully with our children came immediately to mind.

"**P**" pursuit of our **passion** and **purpose**, the impact we make beyond our family. "**I**" **invested** in ourselves. And "**C**" **connected** to a strong support network, so we're in community on our journey. They all came out, within a minute, with clarity and ease at long last.

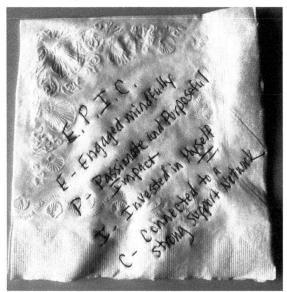

To be clear, I'm not talking about a perfect life, or someone else's version of an E.P.I.C. life… I'm talking about a life filled with the things that matter most to YOU. And one where when things feel out of alignment (which you can expect they will!) you give yourself the grace and space to notice and shift things back to what you really want.

Since then, what I now call the "E.P.I.C. Framework" has become a guiding light in so many ways. It's become the content of my interviews on the podcast, and a focus of my coaching programs. It provides a touchstone for how I'm living my life each day; something I scan for and check-in with myself about during my morning practice. It's a manifesto for living my life. It can be yours too.

E

ENGAGED

You are mindfully engaged with your children and family. You are present and clear about what you think, feel and believe.

P

PURPOSEFUL

You are passionate and purposeful. You use your gifts to make a difference beyond your family.

I

INVESTED

You are invested in
yourself. You make
time for self-care
and learning that
nourishes your mind,
body and spirit.

C

CONNECTED

You are connected
to a strong support
network so you
are in community
throughout your
journey.

MY
Mother's Quest
MANIFESTO

pause to **reflect**

choose myself

IN THE UNEXPECTED CHALLENGES OF
MOTHERHOOD
WE FOUND PARTS OF OURSELVES WE NEVER KNEW EXISTED. BUT, ALSO LOST PARTS OF OURSELVES. AND SIDELINED OUR DREAMS.

make meaning

answer the call

MOTHERHOOD IS A TRANSFORMATIONAL JOURNEY, NOT A DESTINATION. ALONG THE WAY, WE DISCOVER, GROW AND **CHANGE** ALONGSIDE OUR CHILDREN.

deeply rooted

Champion my children

I PAUSED FOR REFLECTION IN A

spark
moment

AS I STOOD AT THE THRESHOLD OF A NEW CHAPTER, I THOUGHT I NEEDED SOMEONE TO OPEN A DOOR FOR ME. THEN, I REALIZED THAT IF I DIDN'T FIRST OPEN THE DOOR...

GIVE MYSELF PERMISSION, AND SAY "YES" TO MYSELF, NO ONE WOULD BE ABLE TO DO THAT FOR ME.

THEN ONE DAY, WE COULD NO LONGER IGNORE THE WHISPERS, WE OPENED OUR EYES AND SAW THE SIGNS ALL AROUND... CHALLENGING US TO CHOOSE OURSELVES.

ongoing
quest

ARE MY MARKERS. I KNOW IF I FOCUS ON THESE, MY LIFE WILL BE FILLED WITH WHAT MATTERS MOST.

I am
the author
of my story

ENGAGE
mindfully with my children

INVEST in myself

Inspiring yet another **generation** to live their E.P.I.C. lives

transformational
journey

live by a set of E.P.I.C. values Deeply rooted, with all of this as my foundation, I choose center-stage of my life.

the E.P.I.C guideposts

PURSUE, PASSIONATE & PURPOSEFUL IMPACT making a difference between my family

CONNECT to a **strong support network** so I am in my community journey

See the signs all around

And one day, when I'm older, perhaps sitting on a porch with my grandchildren, I can tell them all of my stories, and the moments, connections and impact that mattered most.

To answer the call of my

hero's journey

give myself **permission** and say **"yes"** to myself no one would be able to do that for me.
To step into the **fullest expression** of who I'm meant to be

no longer
ignore the
whispers

My Mother's Quest Manifesto

Motherhood is a transformational journey,
not a destination.
Along the way, we discover, grow and change
alongside our children.

In the unexpected challenges of motherhood,
I found parts of myself I never knew existed.
But, also lost parts of myself.
And sidelined my dreams.

Then one day, I could no longer ignore the whispers.
I opened my eyes and saw the signs all around...
challenging me to choose myself.

To step into the fullest expression of who
I'm meant to be.
To answer the call of my own hero's journey.
To become the author of my story.

I paused for reflection in a "spark moment" as I stood
at the threshold of a new chapter.
I thought I needed someone to open a door for me.
Then, I realized that if I didn't first open the door...
give myself permission, and say "yes" to myself,
no one would be able to do that for me.

Today, I'm on an ongoing quest
to live my own unique version of an E.P.I.C. life...
and to inspire and champion my children to do the same.
I know that the impact I seek happens
when I lead the way by my own example.

The E.P.I.C. Guideposts are my markers.
If I focus on these,
my life will be filled with what matters most.
E: Engage mindfully with my children
P: Pursue passionate and purposeful impact,
making a difference beyond my family
I: Invest in myself and
C: Connect to a strong support network
so I am in community on my journey

Deeply rooted, with all of this as my foundation,
I choose center-stage of my life.
And one day, when I'm older,
perhaps sitting on a porch with my grandchildren,
I can tell them all of my stories,
and the moments, connections and impact that mattered
most.
Inspiring yet another generation
to live their E.P.I.C. lives.

ON THE
THRESHOLD

A NEW CHAPTER

On April 15th, 2016, I had a spiritual experience when two birds trapped in my house became my "spark moment" for creating Mother's Quest. I captured my experience and thoughts on a Facebook post that became a declaration, my stake in the ground for a new way of living and a pursuit of my dreams.

Julie Lieberman Neale
April 15, 2016 · 🌐   ...

Friday Philosophical Reflection
Mothers: We Can Be the Hero in Our Own Journeys

Have been dreaming about launching "Mother's Quest" as a social enterprise, with coaching, workshops and summits, a blog and podcast, and eventually a marketplace and venture-fund or foundation...all to support mother's on a quest to become the best mothers they can be, use their unique gifts to make the difference in the world, and invest in and nurture themselves to make those things possible.

Facebook reminded me this morning it was a year ago today that I first invited people to participate in a pilot Mother's Quest workshop. I saw the Facebook memory on my feed and admit I felt a little trapped, frustrated that I haven't taken more action to fulfill this dream.

And then literally moments later this happened...

Jake and I realized that a bird had flown into our house; likely in the short time before we closed the front door after returning from dropping Ryan off at school. The poor bird was frantically flying into windows, moving toward the light but crashing into the glass barrier every time.

At first, we were scared by the thudding of the bird and ran upstairs! But after a few breaths, I realized I just needed to go downstairs and open our back door so it could find its way out. I opened the door, and it was only a few minutes before the bird flew out.

Message from the Universe - Need to Open the Door

Here's the complete text of what I wrote:

"Have been dreaming more about launching "Mother's Quest," a website and social enterprise, with coaching, workshops and retreats, a blog and podcast, and eventually a marketplace and venture-fund...all to support mothers on a quest to become the best mothers they can be, use their unique gifts to make the difference in the world, and invest in and nurture themselves to make those things possible.

Facebook reminded me this morning that it was a year

ago today since I first invited people to participate in a pilot Mother's Quest workshop. I saw the "Memory" on my feed and admit I felt trapped, frustrated that I haven't taken more action to fulfill this dream.

*And then literally moments later this happened...
My three-year old son Jake and I realized that a bird had flown into our house. The poor bird was frantically flying into windows, moving toward the light but crashing into the glass barrier every time. At first, we were scared by the thudding of the bird and ran upstairs. But after a few breaths, I realized I just needed to go down and open our back door so it could find its way. I opened the door, and it was less than a minute before the bird flew out.*

MESSAGE FROM THE UNIVERSE– OPEN THE DOOR

I stood at the door and thought fleetingly that perhaps this was a message from the universe. The bird was a fitting metaphor for where I am in my quest to create this enterprise right now. I try moving toward a bright vision, but feel like I keep crashing against barriers, and may need someone to open a door for me.

I watched the bird that escaped as it walked around my back porch. For some reason, it wasn't flying away. I wondered whether it had injured a wing. Then, I heard flapping again, and realized there was a second bird trapped inside. It was as if the other bird was waiting for the one inside before it would take flight. I opened the door again, and the second bird hopped right out. To make sure I hadn't imagined the whole thing,

I took a photo of the bird walking out and of the two birds perched together afterwards on a nearby tree.

I decided the universe didn't believe I got the message the first time and so sent it again to drive the point. I figured I better sit down, write the story and share it. Only as I began typing the story, did I realize there was another message that the second bird was delivering. No one else is going to open a door for me, until I open the door myself.

MOTHERS TOO CAN ANSWER THE CALL

I have been reading a lot about the "Hero's Journey," inspired to learn more by a conversation between author Elizabeth Gilbert and Oprah on my favorite show, "Super Soul Sunday." Joseph Campbell, famed anthropologist, says there are key elements to every journey, including the moment when the hero answers the "call" and when the hero finds the needed mentors to help light the way along the arduous journey.

He believed only men need to take this journey; women, as the child-birthing nurturers, have already arrived at the destination for which the men are searching. But, I agree with Maureen Murdock, who in her book, "The Heroine's Journey," refutes this notion and believes women have a quest of their own to take.

Today, I commit to answering the call. To take bold action and provide a living example to myself, other women, and my children that mothers too can and should be the hero in our own journeys."

This experience highlighted two important practices that I've circled back to again and again:

PRACTICE #1
PLANT SEEDS

Sometimes, when we are on the threshold of a new chapter, and seek dramatic changes in our lives, we don't realize that in small, incremental ways, we've already planted seeds for our future.

The day the two birds were trapped in my home acted as a catalyst. But, there were choices I made that enabled that spark moment to become possible. I planted a seed when I had the courage to lead my first Mother's Quest Workshop.

I planted a seed when I decided to listen intently to Elizabeth Gilbert on Oprah's Super Soul Sunday talk about the hero's journey. I planted a seed when shortly after, I chose to attend an Elizabeth Gilbert Writer's Workshop, a 44th birthday present to myself and wrote a letter of permission that set the stage for what came a year later.

We may not realize it, but these little moments of choosing ourselves, when given space and time to germinate, result in visible new growth.

PERMISSION

Dear Julie,

I am your Principal. I am the Chief Architect. I am designing your life. I already have the blueprints. You should know, you are living and will live a blessed and rich and memorable and meaningful life. Your design is one of connection and love, of challenge and perseverence, of stepping into your authenticity and your gifts. You will not settle for anything less than absolutely everything... that matters to you. [Stay awake] You have the right and the obligation to live your life to its fullest.

The original "Letter of Permission" I wrote to myself at Elizabeth Gilbert's Creative Writing Retreat that planted the seeds for Mother's Quest

Find books, movies, songs that connect you to a topic that has been calling to you.

Spend some time visualizing what you seek. Allow yourself to feel what it would be like when that goal is realized.

Think about something you've always wanted to do and pilot it on a smaller scale.

GO DEEPER

Listen to my introductory episode for more about the seeds I planted that brought me to living my E.P.I.C. Life.

Hear actress, author and activist Tembi Locke talk about the seeds planted in her creative life through her family lineage and upbringing.

Listen to my father David Lieberman talk about the moments and experiences where he planted seeds by pursuing his fate.

What's something you've been longing for?

How can you take one small step toward experiencing what you seek?

PRACTICE #2
FOLLOW THE SIGNS

When we're on the threshold of a new chapter, I believe those seeds we plant begin to take root, present themselves in our lives in unexpected ways, and call us to something greater. What begins as a whisper, gets louder until, like that quote shared by Anaïs Nin the time comes "When the risk to remain tight in a bud was more painful than the risk it took to blossom."

If when presented with signs in our lives, like I was with the two birds trapped in my house, and we slow down enough to pause and make meaning of them, as I did when I stood at the doorway, we can use the experiences in our lives as a catalyst to answer the call to our own hero's journey.

Synchronicity

The day after the Charlottesville rally, I knew I could no longer stay silent about racism and bigotry in our country and I determined that I would use the podcast to shine a light on social justice issues. I was in Santa Barbara at the time celebrating my anniversary with my husband Chris. We were getting ready to go sit by the pool together, but I told him to go ahead and I stayed in the hotel room to type out a Facebook post with my commitment.

That day, the Women Podcasters in Solidarity Initiative was born. Soon after, I interviewed diversity, equity and inclusion expert Nicole Lee, a human rights attorney who had been on the ground in Ferguson providing counsel and then Sara Mokuria of Mothers Against Police Brutality, in an episode dedicated by Collette Flanagan, the founder of the organization.

Because of the steps I took in speaking out, months later, I was invited to speak on a panel at a conference about my experience, where Collette Flanagan happened to be the keynote speaker. During a break, the two of us found quiet time to talk together and conspire about how to create change and got our photo taken together. It was the start of a relationship that continues today.

It wasn't until I drove home to the S.F. Bay Area from the conference that I realized the synchronicity...it was the exact same hotel in Santa Barbara, celebrating my anniversary with my husband, where I declared my commitment to anti-racism and then found myself speaking on a panel and talking with Collette months later. I took this as a sign. I was on an important and aligned path and I needed to keep taking steps ahead.

Julie Lieberman Neale
August 12, 2017 · 🌐

On this day, a year ago, I learned that my childhood friend Leslie Rabinovitz Fischer passed away in the night after a three year battle with pancreatic cancer.

I sat down that morning to reflect on the lessons Leslie gave me about how to live my life and wrote the words that became the mantra that closes every Mother's Quest Podcast Episode, "Seize the day, love your people, honor your gifts."

I also wrote that there is no time for "bullshit." There's nothing like seeing your friend face mortality to put things in perspective.

This morning, a year later, I woke up to devastating news again. News about white supremacists marching in Virginia with torches and Nazi salutes.

My experience losing Leslie, and the messages that have become mantras, inspire me to move past my own "bullshit" today and into action...past my own limiting beliefs that I can't really make a difference, that if I speak out in any way I'll just say the wrong thing or do more harm, that I can't handle the harsh judgement (on either side) from being visible on an issue like racism and police brutality.

Many may have seen posts from me in previous months, or listened to my conversations on the podcast about an initiative I'm working on to raise awareness and funds related to Black Lives Matter.

The initiative is not perfectly planned yet. I'm still trying to find guests for my podcast, speakers for my bay area event, and to find a fiscal sponsor for the Mother's Quest Giving Fund. And, I haven't officially invited other women podcasters to pledge to be a part.

But, what I'm waking up to this morning, with my memory of Leslie's life lessons and the horrific news of yesterday, is there's no time to wait. It will never be perfect. And, I want to be part of some positive action today in response to yesterday's ugliness.

If you are a women podcaster with a platform and want to be part of the initiative, "Women Podcasters in Solidarity," visit www.mothersquest.com/solidarity to sign up. I envision this as a seasonal initiative with the first focus being on Black Lives Matter.

If you're a mother working on the frontlines of this issue and you're open to helping to educate and raise awareness OR a mother who wants to learn, message me and sign up at www.mothersquest.com for email updates.

Appreciate any help spreading the word...

"Seize the day, honor your gifts, love your people." And, expand that definition of what "your people" really means.

Create more opportunities for pause and stillness in your life so you can slow down enough to get present with the feelings in your body and desires of your heart.

Pay attention to the unexpected or serendipitous moments in your life, and with curiosity, ask yourself what meaning they might have.

GO DEEPER

Listen to my conversation with Rachel Macy Stafford about the "spark moment" she had on a run that became a sign for change.

Hear Dr. Song talk about her epic journey and the Stanford mind body medicine conference that pointed her on her unique path as a holistic pediatrician.

When you allow yourself to get quiet, what whispers call you to something greater?

What truth about your becoming have you been ignoring?

What unexpected recent experiences might have deeper meaning for you in your life?

E
ENGAGED

Mindfully engaging with our children, for me, means that we bring thoughtfulness, intention and presence to how we interact with our children, that we see them and embrace them for who they are, and that we allow ourselves to engage in a reciprocal relationship with them, knowing that they can bring as much wisdom and insight to us as we strive to bring to them.

PRACTICE #3
MAKE SPACE FOR
MINDFULNESS

Ever notice how the smallest moments or routines often bring the most powerful connection between you and your children? In our rush to get from point A to point B, we can forget to slow down, create pockets of quality time, and notice the thoughts, feelings and experiences that are the fabric of our E.P.I.C. lives. When we consciously create space for mindfulness, we increase appreciation, insight and understanding.

The Gratitude Jar

One of my favorite ways to build mindfulness with my family is through our Gratitude Jar. For five years now, we will gather up during a meal, and write a few things we are grateful for on a slip of paper, then share and toss it into our big glass jar. Over the years, we have had as much fun reaching down deep and reminding ourselves of our gratitude from the past as we enjoy writing what's present for us today. So many little moments that would otherwise pass us right by, have been captured on these slips of paper. Perspective, mindfulness, and growing gratitude all with this simple ritual!

Grow your gratitude by being mindful of and naming the things you're grateful for. Sharing yourself is as important as asking your children.

Take advantage of mealtime, car rides and bedtime to create opportunities for inquiry. Allow space for mutual discovery. Listen to what's bubbling up for your children. Ask your children for advice in your life.

Listen to Nancy Netherland share about the way she creates space for gratitude with her children, even in the midst of their chronic illnesses.

Hear partners Lynn Johnson and Allison Kenny talk about bringing mindfulness to parenting through their "Go Girl Culture Code."

Uncover tools and practices to bring mindfulness even in the middle of the chaos with Michelle Gale.

What special rituals to enhance mindfulness and connection could you build into your family routines?

When are the natural moments in your day when your children are open and receptive to sharing with you? How could you create more space around those moments to be fully present?

PRACTICE #4
DO SOMETHING
TOGETHER

A few years ago, I brought my teen son Ryan, at first a reluctant guest, to a Youth Speaks event in San Francisco. It didn't take long for Ryan to open up to the incredible spoken word poetry. As he watched and listened to young people, of different ethnicities, sexual orientations, religions, and abilities, speak about their lived experience, I could feel the experience striking Ryan deeply, opening a new awareness in him. And then, he turned to me and said "Never stop taking me to things like this." This is just one example of many things I consciously choose to do with my children. From Adventure Fridays at the Square Peg Ranch and taking an art journaling class with my youngest Jacob, to recording a special podcast episode at a sound recording studio and co-facilitating an Election Candidate Q & A with Ryan, shared experiences expand our learning and bring us together in powerful ways.

Ryan and I getting ready to record our episode together at a sound recording studio In San Francisco.

Jacob and I enjoying the horses during our Adventure Friday at Square Peg Ranch.

Think about something that you enjoy doing and invite your children to join alongside you. Conversely, follow your own child's lead, joining them in something that lights them up.

Engage with your children in service or other meaningful experiences that will expand their awareness, competence and contribution.

Listen to Ryan and I reflect together after taking a special Milestone Hike on his 13th birthday.

Hear from activist Paola Mendoza about how she makes special time with her son through "Adventure Fridays."

Learn about engaging our children in service with California Volunteers Leader Karen Baker.

QUESTIONS FOR REFLECTION

What is something you love to do that you'd like to share with your children?

Where are there opportunities in your own community or in your work to meaningfully engage your children?

PRACTICE #5
HAVE A COURAGEOUS
CONVERSATION

One of the biggest gifts I received from diversity, equity and inclusion coach and human rights attorney Nicole Lee, from our conversation on the podcast, was the encouragement to hold a "growth mindset" vs. a fixed mindset when approaching courageous conversations with our children about complex issues like race, sex, religion and more. With a growth mindset... instead of shying away from or "shushing" our kids when they ask questions, or say something that concerns us, we can release striving for perfection, or "getting things right" and instead stay open. Other conversations, with Boys & Sex Author Peggy Orenstein, and Raising Luminaries Ashia Ray, also helped me realize the critical role I play through conversation with my children to deepen our learning together on issues that matter.

My husband exploring inclusivity with Jacob through the powerful book "Best in Me" by Natalie McDonald-Perkins.

Let your kids know you welcome their honest questions and thoughts on issues like race. Also be vulnerable yourself and willing to share your own beliefs, mistakes, and experiences.

Find opportunities in daily situations to spark conversation. Then create opportunities for reflection by utilizing books and movies and exploring them together.

GO DEEPER

Listen to Nicole Lee shine light on how to approach conversations about race with our children.

Learn about the importance of talking with our boys about sex, even if it's uncomfortable, with best-selling author Peggy Orenstein.

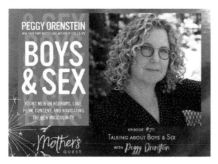

Explore neurodiversity and how to use the power of books to smash the kyriarchy with Ashia Ray of Raising Luminaries.

What blocks or biases of your own might you need to unpack or examine in order to lean into courageous conversation with your children?

What experiences, challenges or stories in your own life could you share with your children that might create an opening for conversation?

PRACTICE #6
STEP UP STEP BACK

When I worked at the youth development organization, Alternatives in Action, and we would set group agreements with the young people, one of my favorite agreements was "Step Up Step Back."

This idea, that sometimes we need to step up and share more fully or be more vocal, and that sometimes we might need to step back and create more space, can be powerfully applied to parenthood. I notice again and again, that sometimes I need to be more present in my children's lives, set more boundaries, provide more structure and support. And other times, what's needed is to fade back, release expectations, and create room for failure.

mothersquestpod

Hey mom (and other Neale's)! I landed safely and am having a lot of fun. Thank you for letting me do this!!! Ill try to keep in touch a little. Enjoy the free time, and I love you

Love you s😊 much. Proud of you. Have a great time!!

Also go to bed

mothersquestpod Another E.P.I.C. snapshot moment and text from Ryan, sent at 12:30 am. His best friend moved to Seattle and last night he flew on his own, unassisted, to visit him. Apparently they were up until the middle of the night catching up, laughing and telling stories.
..
..
There are so many things I love about this experience...
✨ The friendship between these two boys developed over years, in good times and bad
✨ How independent Ryan felt to find his way through security and onto the plane on his own
✨ The joy on his face in this snapshot his friend's Mom sent me when they saw each other
✨ The appreciation in Ryan's text to me
..
..
Navigating the social scene and new challenges of high school and adolescence is no small thing. I appreciate moments like these when things feel easy and right. Bottling up this goodness!!

Notice when you're holding tightly to your own expectations for your children and remind yourself that your children are on their own journey.

Pay attention to when your children are struggling or asking for help. Think about how you can bring more presence or provide structures and supports in an empowering way.

GO DEEPER

Listen to Debbie Reber talk about how surrender helped her differently-wired son and her thrive.

Learn from former Stanford Dean Julie Lythcott-Haims about how to raise adults by moving our egos out of the way and allowing our children space to grow.

Hear about the ways that Judy Blank stepped up to advocate and champion her trans daughter Corey Rae.

When do you notice it is important to step in more fully with your children?

How do you view failure? What would happen if you give your children the opportunity to fail?

We cannot live our children's lives for them. They have to "choose in" for themselves.

CLOSING

Photo: Roger Jordan

Putting It All Together

Four Practices To Help You
"E" Engage Mindfully
With Your Children

Create Space for Mindfulness

Do Something Together

Have a Courageous Conversation

Step Up Step Back

PLANTING INTENTIONS

I've learned again and again that a good metaphor always helps us make meaning. So, I invite you to reflect on the stories, examples and practices in this Mother's Quest Inspiration Guide Vol. 1 and then think about what intentions you might like to "plant" so that they can take root in your life.

Just as we unknowingly plant seeds that bring unexpected growth to our future, we can also consciously plant intentions, and purposefully integrate new ways of thinking and being into our lives, starting today.

During the Mother's Quest Circle, my signature Spark Your E.P.I.C. Life Group Coaching Series, we each select one intention to "plant" during our time together.

Mother's Quest Circle Members "plant intentions" as part of the four-session Spark Your E.P.I.C. Life Coaching Series

We then get clear about what that intention will need to be nourished and grow, just as we would need clarity about the water, sunlight and soil a new plant needs to flourish. We call these "care instructions" and keep them at the forefront as a commitment to ourselves.

Before you set this book down, I'd love for you to plant at least one intention and create some care instructions of your own to nurture that intention.

I COMMIT TO PLANT THIS INTENTION

_____

_____

_____

MY CARE INSTRUCTIONS FOR THIS INTENTION

CARE & MAINTENANCE

TINY PRACTICES MAKE
A BIG DIFFERENCE

I hope the exploration of my journey the last four years, the practices that guided me when I was "on the threshold" of a new chapter, and the four I highlighted for meaningfully engaging with our children, spark some ideas to help you more fully live your E.P.I.C. Life.

I also hope you realize that a life filled with the things that matter most is already available to you. And that small practices, often of things you already know but easily forget in the busyness of life, can make a big difference. To seal this awareness, I wanted to leave you with a few more bite-sized E.P.I.C. invitations, inspired by conversations on the podcast. Ten in fact!

1

When you first wake up, put one hand on your heart, put one hand on your belly, close your eyes and just ask yourself, what do I need today?

Ep. 63 A Maker's Journey to a Good Life with Jonathan Fields

2

Turn an ordinary task with your child into a song

Ep. 38 Making Space and Finding Rhythm with "Kindie Rock" Star Laurie Berkner

3

Take a moment to lie flat on your back

Ep. 59 The Healer Lies Within Through Ayurveda with Avanti Kumar Singh

4

Meet someone new and be the first one to say hello and to really see the humanity in them

Ep. 75 A Call for Kinetic Partnership with While Black's Darius Hicks

5

Ask your child a question and wait for the answer

Ep.70 Blazing a Transgender Trail with Corey Rae and Her Mother Judy Blank

Ten Tiny Practices That Can Make a Big Difference in your E.P.I.C. Life

6 *Pause and reflect before rushing to resolution*

Ep. 65 The Power of Being Seen & The Spiral Path with Amy Simpkins

7 *Reveal a personal flaw to your child*

Encore Episode: "Flawed" with Truth Bomb Mom Kristina Kuzmic

8 *Read a book by an author of color*

Ep. 66 A Love Letter to Friendship with Desiree Adaway and Pamela Slim

9 *Take three deep breaths and then ask yourself "What matters most now?"*

Ep. 51 Equanimity & The Calm in the Storm with Mindful Parent Michelle Gale

10 *Break bread with someone different from you*

Ep. 12 Breaking Bread and Building Bridges with Saadia Ahmed

AN OPEN INVITATION

I look forward to sharing Vol. 2 of the Inspiration Guide Series on the next E.P.I.C. Guidepost "P" all about pursuing our passionate and purposeful impact in the world beyond our family. Until then, I hope you'll connect more deeply with the Mother's Quest Community. Here are a few ways:

 Subscribe to the Mother's Quest Podcast on any of your favorite podcast apps, so each new episode will download directly to you. You are also always welcome to email me to let me know what you're most on a quest for, and I'll select an episode that might light your way.

✉ julie@mothersquest.com
Or you can view the episodes yourself
🎤 www.mothersquest.com/podcast

 Sign up for the Mother's Quest email list and you'll receive reflections from my life, invitations, announcements, and show notes for new episodes.

✉ www.mothersquest.com

You can also follow us on social media
⬛ mothersquestpod
f mothersquest

Visit our MemberVault site for access to Mother's Quest resources and self-guided courses. There you can also sign up for one-on-one coaching or to participate in an upcoming Mother's Quest Circle.
🌐 https://mothersquest.vipmembervault.com/

 And finally, you can join the Mother's Quest Community on Facebook for opportunities to share and learn from one another through structured virtual gatherings, posts and lives from our monthly Ambassadors, and weekly threads that have us reflecting.
🌐 www.mothersquest.com/community

Look forward to connecting with you in whatever ways call to you!

With love and so much appreciation,

ACKNOWLEDGEMENTS

There are no words to fully capture the appreciation I have for my family (especially my husband Chris and my children Ryan and Jacob), my friends, members of the Mother's Quest team, and the guides, podcast guests, and Mother's Quest Community members who sometimes light the way and sometimes follow my lead on this journey. It's your insight, love and wisdom that help me reveal new layers of what it means to live an E.P.I.C. life and recommit to my Mother's Quest Manifesto again and again. I am forever grateful to travel with you.

This Inspiration Guide would not have been possible without the genius of Alexandra Franzen and Lindsey Smith who created the Tiny Book Course. Thank you to Mother's Quest community members Rigette, Jen and Remee who worked on the design, provided editing and gave valuable feedback. Finally, I want to extend special appreciation to Jenjii, Cameron, Leslie, Lena and Heather who all said "yes" to bringing their beautiful book dreams forward in this first, but certainly not the last, Mother's Quest Tiny Book Course cohort.

Don't Go
Back to old habits and thoughts that strain and constrain
To a former version of self that felt small and safe in hiding
Don't Go
Quiet, unsure of voice and what there is to say or if there is anything to
say at all
Don't Go
Completely still, unable to act, paralyzed by guilt or grief or fear of doing
more harm than good.
Instead...
Go Boldly
Rooted in a knowing that you matter and can be a force for change.
Go Compassionately
Connected to a belief that we are more bound together than divided by
difference
Go Persistently
One tiny step at a time if you need.
But Keep Going .
Evolving, learning, dreaming, hoping
Until you realize that there is no destination
Just the knowing of the journey itself
Ever widening and lighting the way before you.

Mother's Quest member Jena Schwartz encouraged me to write poetry!
This first poem, which I wrote in February 2019, is dedicated to all of us... to
encourage us to stay on the path toward our E.P.I.C. lives.

An integral part of living an E.P.I.C. life?

You inspire everyone around you, including your children, to grow into their best selves.